...a season of
Stillness

...a season of

Stillness

ELIZABETH M. HOEKSTRA
WITH THE WATERCOLORS OF MARLENE McLOUGHLIN

CROSSWAY BOOKS • WHEATON, ILLINOIS
A DIVISION OF GOOD NEWS PUBLISHERS

Cover and interior illustrations: Marlene McLoughlin

Book Design: Liita Forsyth

Hand-tooled leather for cover: Bob Roberts

First printing 2000

Printed in the United States of America

Library of Congress Cataloging-in-Publication Data
Hoekstra, Elizabeth M. 1962-
   A season of stillness / Elizabeth M. Hoekstra.
      p.   cm. (All creation sings)
    ISBN 1-58134-204-7 (alk. paper)
    1. Meditations. 2. Winter—Religious aspects—Christianity—Meditations.
I. Title.
BV4832.2.H597   2000
242—dc21
                                      00-009046
                                        CIP

15	14	13	12	11	10	09	08	07	06	05	04	03	02	01	00
15	14	13	12	11	10	9	8	7	6	5	4	3	2	1	

Dedication

To my grandparents,
Ted and Mimi Day,
for modeling a love for God's earth

We can see parallels between the seasons in nature and the seasons in our faith journeys. The winter snows on our small New Hampshire farm remind me of the blanket of God's love and grace for us. For my husband, Peter, our children, Geneva and Jordan, and me, this season of stillness finds us feeling grateful for the Lord's abiding faithfulness. In the following reflections on God's ways as revealed in the events and residents of our home and farm, we hope you find a measure of peace and encouragement to trust the Lord in each season of your life.

Come Enjoy Peace with Us

FROM WHOSE WOMB comes the ice? Who gives birth to the frost from the heavens when the waters become hard as stone, when the surface of the deep is frozen? Can you bind the beautiful Pleiades? Can you loose the cords of Orion? Can you bring forth the constellations in their seasons or lead out the Bear with its cubs? Do you know the laws of the heavens? Can you set up God's dominion over the earth?

Job 38:29-33

The Lord Is Strong

You, O God, are strong.

PSALM 62:11b

Good Fruit

But the fruit of the Spirit is love, joy, peace, patience, kindness, goodness, faithfulness, gentleness and self-control.

GALATIANS 5:22-23a

THE JANUARY DAY felt bleak and cold when a special delivery box arrived at our house. Any package post-Christmas feels even more special. Oranges and grapefruit came into view as my children and I lifted the lid of a carton sent from Florida. The colorful fruit was a feast for my color-starved eyes. We all squealed with delight.

Until that moment my soul had felt as bleak as the midwinter New England day. I felt oppressed by the bitter cold and relentless gray clouds. The children sensed my chilled heart and had been squabbling. As we fingered the fruit, I felt the Lord nudge my heart: *Remember the fruit of the Spirit?* I began to tick them off in my mind, trying to recount them all: *Love, joy, peace, patience, kindness....* Oops! We hadn't been faithful in practicing them that day!

Later, after we had tasted the fruit, I looked up the verses about the fruit of the Spirit. Paul, writing to the churches in Galatia (Gal. 5:22), used a singular word for fruit. It's not *fruits* of the Spirit, but rather *the fruit* of the Spirit—one fruit made up of nine segments like an orange. I understood that each aspect of the spiritual fruit was like one of the segments that contribute to the whole orange.

With this fruit we can't choose which attributes we might like. "Oh, I think I'll choose joy and peace, but I'm not into patience or self-control today!" It's an all-or-nothing fruit. The deeper side is that each segment is a characteristic of Christ. As we become more Christlike, we can be confident of His fruit and His Spirit in our lives.

The fruit of the Spirit is a gift—a gift of grace that affects our attitudes and relationships. And just as the gift box of fruit brought joy to that January day, so can God's fruit in me produce joy to pass on to others.

MORE SCRIPTURE FOR STUDY:
Matthew 7:9-12, 15-20; John 15:1-16;
James 1:17-18; 2 Peter 1:5-8

Standing Ready

Preach the Word; be prepared in season
and out of season.

2 TIMOTHY 4:2a

EVERYTHING SEEMS "out of season" in the winter months of New England. My favorite produce (fresh berries and vegetables), my favorite activity (horseback riding), and my family's favorite relaxation activities (boating and swimming) all take place during a *different* season.

Sometimes I need to remind myself of what I *do* enjoy about the winter season: skiing, sledding, hot chocolate, a break from farm repair work. I really do like the winter months; still I'm always anxious for the next season to arrive. Yet each season is only three months!

Don't we at times bring that same impatience to our faith? I'm anxious to get beyond whatever lesson the Lord is leading me through. I want to "arrive" at the destination He's bringing me to. But we won't arrive at a final resting spot in our faith until we die. On this side of heaven there is always more for us to learn in our journey with the Lord.

Ecclesiastes 3 talks about all of the "seasons" humankind encounters. Just a few are "a time to be born and a time to die, … a time to tear down and a time to build, … a time to mourn and a time to dance, … a time to be silent and a time to speak, a time to love and a time to hate" (3:1-8a). In which "season" are you? Like me, are you anxious to move on to the next season?

Paul's words above from 2 Timothy remind us to be patient in or out of season. Perhaps he meant "in season" as a time of joy and contentment and "out of season" as a time of discouragement. But he still says to be "prepared." Prepared for what? My pastor answered this question with the comment, "I'm always prepared to preach, pray, or die." I like that response. It's exactly what Paul was talking about—be ready for the unexpected.

Whether you are feeling in season or out, pray that your heart will be prepared for the Lord's next call or move on your life. I want to be ready. Don't you?

MORE SCRIPTURE FOR STUDY:
Ecclesiastes 2:24-26; 3:1-14;
2 Timothy 4:1-8; 1 Peter 3:13-16

A Straight Track

In all your ways acknowledge him, and he will
make your paths straight.

PROVERBS 3:6

I AWOKE ONE WINTER MORNING and saw that six inches of snow had fallen during the night. I love waking up to a fresh snowfall. Through the kitchen window all the evergreens looked weighted with new clothes. In the driveway car tracks, boot marks, ski lines, and dog prints had disappeared under the white cover.

As I stepped through the snow, I saw a fresh line of canine tracks leading up the trail behind our house. *Dog, fox, or coyote?* I wondered. I looked closer at the size of the padded footprints and the spread between the strides. The long length of leg, big paw, and spread toes indicated that the animal had to be a dog or coyote. Then I remembered the dead giveaway for distinguishing between dog tracks and coyote tracks.

A domesticated dog's tracks are aimless and distracted. His prints usually move from tree to tree. They cut back, circle around, and retrace themselves. Why? Supper is at home. He doesn't need to hunt; he's "just checking." But a coyote's tracks run as straight as a compass needle. The marks are perfectly measured with a clear destination in mind. Coyotes don't waste energy or time snuffling around trees just for fun.

I followed the tracks in the new snow. They were straight and true in the center of the trail until it curved out of sight at a bend. I probably could have set a yardstick to it. This was one intent coyote.

The verse above came to mind. "He will make your paths straight" or as the King James Version says, "He shall direct thy paths." Sounds like the straight route of the undistracted coyote, doesn't it? At times, however, we have a tendency to be like a domesticated dog with a barking-up-the-wrong-tree approach to our days. Our attentions are split between all of our time demands.

Proverbs 15:21b says, "A man of understanding keeps a straight course." A man or woman who is clear on his or her path, its destination, and the hoped-for reward isn't distracted by items along the periphery of the path. He or she knows to simply follow the Lord's leading, which avoids detours, confusion, and getting lost.

Will you journey with me as we follow our Lord's path?

MORE SCRIPTURE FOR STUDY:
Deuteronomy 5:32-33; Psalm 27:11;
Proverbs 4:25-27; Matthew 7:13-14

A Flame of Invitation

No one lights a lamp and hides it in a jar or puts it under a bed.
Instead, he puts it on a stand, so that those who come in
can see the light.

LUKE 8:16

MY THUMBNAIL PRIED up the buildup of wax on the windowsill of my friend's historic home. Even as the wax flaked away, the wooden sill remained stained and gouged from other scratch marks. I thought of the candles that had burned in the windows of this eighteenth-century New England home, some made of talo (animal fat and unbearably smoky). A flame in the front window usually says, "Hello! We're here. Come in. Won't you join us?" One flickering light, one tiny gesture of hospitality had opened the door to fellowship over the years.

I love to light candles in my home. I like the big triple-wicked round ones that have a pine or floral aroma. I light them at the end of the day near dusk and frequently breathe a prayer: *Lord, let me be a light in my own home to my family or to any friends who might stop by. I pray that this representative flame of You in my life would reach beyond these walls.*

Have you prayed a similar prayer? Do you have a visible flicker of God's light in your soul? Does your relationship with the Lord shine from your eyes and act as an invitation for people to talk with you? Does God's flame in you draw people in to Him?

Matthew records Jesus' words: "In the same way, let your light shine before men, that they may see your good deeds and praise your Father in heaven" (5:16). The purpose of lit candles in homestead windows was an open invitation; the purpose of God's light in our lives is also an open invitation. It invites searching, road-weary people into God's house. Won't you ignite the wick in your soul today to guide and welcome someone?

MORE SCRIPTURE FOR STUDY:
Psalms 18:28; 19:8; Matthew 5:13-16; 2 Corinthians 4:1-6

Caring Provision

My God will meet all your needs according to his glorious riches in Christ Jesus.

PHILIPPIANS 4:19

MY HUSBAND, PETER, was in Russia—gone far from home yet again. Even though we talked every other day by phone, the distance between us made me feel uncared for. He couldn't help with the snowstorm from yesterday that had dumped two feet of snow that turned to ice today because of rain.

The plowed driveway looked like a downhill toboggan run. I felt trapped in my house, able to walk outside only if I stayed along the crunchy edges of the driveway. Forget trying to drive anywhere. The sand truck I'd called hours ago apparently had other, more important people to tend to.

Glancing out of the kitchen window, hoping to see the sand truck, I was instead greeted by a flock of dripping wet turkeys. Fifteen of them stalked with an ungainly gait across a small clearing, pausing here and there to peck at something. What, I wondered, were they possibly finding to eat along the snow-and-ice covered ground and branches? Then I saw that they had stopped at the barberry bushes poking up through the snow. Until that moment I had thought the branches were bare except for a few thorns. But then I saw the bright red berries. The turkeys meticulously plucked them clean and then moved out of sight.

"Look at the birds of the air; they do not sow or reap … and yet your heavenly Father feeds them" (Matt. 6:26a). Once again the Lord poignantly reminded me of His tender love. How could I possibly continue to feel uncared for with the evidence of His Word right outside my window? "Are you not much more valuable than they?" (6:26b). I knew then that the One who really cared was the only One who really mattered.

Will you join me today and thank Him for the perfect timing of His provision? Accept the absolute assurance He offers us and pray:

I trust to see Your goodness, Lord,
in whatever this day may bring.

MORE SCRIPTURE FOR STUDY:
Psalms 37:3-5; 121; Matthew 6:25-34;
Philippians 4:6-7; 1 Peter 5:6-7

Step by Step

Since we live by the Spirit, let us keep in step with the Spirit.

GALATIANS 5:25

A NUMBER OF YEARS AGO I joined my mother and a few of her friends for a day of cross-country skiing. We met at a nearby mountain. Feeling energetic, we decided to ski up the mountain, have lunch at the top, then enjoy a brisk swoosh down. I felt game for the idea, pushing a brief thought to the back of my mind about having worked a long and difficult night at my hospital nursing job just a few hours before.

The trail crisscrossed the lower edges of the mountain, but soon took a decidedly upward turn. Our pace slowed. We clambered over snow-covered, downed trees, around rocks, and steadily made our way up—more by side-stepping and V-step herringbone than by actual skiing.

Our breath quickened. Just as the final push above the tree line was in sight, utter exhaustion overcame me. My arms ached from the strain, my legs burned, and my lungs couldn't seem to get enough air. I couldn't keep up with the other women—and they were at least twenty-five years older than I was!

I felt humiliated. Subconsciously, I began to look at my skis rather than at the women in front of me or at my destination. I counted each ski-step up to twenty, then started over. Step by step I finally joined the other women at the top and felt a renewed burst of energy at the view of the southern White Mountains—snowed-covered, but sharp and brilliant in the sunlight. I thought, *So this is what a mountaintop experience feels like. The high seems higher after you've experienced a low.*

My methodical step-by-step movement brought me to the top of that exhausting mountain. As the above verse infers, our walk with the Lord is a step-by-step process too. We don't just cruise smoothly along. We are to match our strides step by step with the Holy Spirit. There will be times when our journeys will seem laborious and humbling. But each step, each lesson learned takes us closer to the heart of our Lord. Aren't you glad to know that our final destination will be worth the climb?

MORE SCRIPTURE FOR STUDY:
Proverbs 14:15; Isaiah 42:10-11;
Micah 4:1-2; 6:8; Romans 5:1-6

Mining Gold

There is a mine for silver and a place where gold is refined....
He searches the sources of the rivers and brings
hidden things to light.

JOB 28:1, 11

WHO AMONG US wouldn't love to discover a vein of gold or silver? Wouldn't we set to mining it, perhaps abandoning reason in the hope of buried treasure?

Such was the thought when gold allegedly was discovered early in this century in the town where I live. Investors were captivated with high hopes of a lucrative gold mine. The mine was built and men were hired for the back-breaking task of mining. The shaft crept deeper and deeper into the earth. But soon afterward, the apparent vein still had yet to yield a significant amount of gold. Was it a heist or had there really been gold?

The story has made me wonder why God created gold to run in veins underground. Gold has long been a universal currency. Is it valuable because it's so hard to get out of the ground? God could have made it grow on trees. I think therein lies the answer to why the Lord put gold in the ground. Gold parallels where the gold is in our souls: deep in our hearts. It's hard to get to. Sometimes He has to chip away at our hardened hearts to mine it out.

The above verse tells us that He "brings hidden things to light." What hidden things? There are two really. One is the hidden rock-hard stubbornness we find in our hearts that needs to be confessed before it can be discarded. The second hidden thing is the gold beneath that layer of stone. Our gentle Lord, after first removing the flint from our hearts, reaches in and very gently exposes the gold imbedded there. He "brings [it] to light."

Job said, "When he has tested me, I will come forth as gold" (23:10). When we "come forth as gold," we reflect God's iridescent light.

MORE SCRIPTURE FOR STUDY:
Job 28:1-11; Psalm 51:10; Luke 6:43-45;
James 4:8

Show and Tell

*How useless to spread a net in full view
of all the birds!*

PROVERBS 1:17

ONE WINTER DAY my children created homemade traps to fend off boredom. I'm uncertain of what they hoped to catch or if they really cared whether or not they caught anything. Their efforts seemed more focused on the process of developing the right trigger with enough sensitivity to snap the trap. They experimented outside with their traps while the chipmunks, squirrels, and chickadees scolded overhead in the trees and bird feeders.

The above verse, which I've always found humorous, came to mind. I wondered whether or not birds, chipmunks, or squirrels have enough common sense to "see" and figure out a trap that has been set. They are watchful, but I suspect that their timidity is more from the human smell than the actual trap.

Humans, like birds, are wary. New Englanders tend to be overly suspicious of others' motives. This dubious nature makes New Englanders some of the most difficult people to evangelize. Stoic and self-sufficient, they tend to not feel the *need* for the Lord.

I've learned that the best way to tell people about the Lord is to *show* them. Some call it "friendship evangelism." As the above verse suggests, we can't hope to "trap" people into Christianity. Witnessing works in subtle ways. As our lives reflect our likeness to Christ, others will be drawn closer.

Don't you want your life to reflect Christ? Don't you want your actions to speak louder than your words? This week practice showing evangelism in a unique way for a friend who may be searching. You might send an encouraging card, cook a dessert to share, or go for a walk together. Let your kind actions show Christ.

MORE SCRIPTURE FOR STUDY:
Proverbs 12:14-28; Acts 1:8;
1 Corinthians 10:31-11:1;
2 Corinthians 4:1-6

Joy in Trials

Consider it pure joy, my brothers, whenever you face trials
of many kinds, because you know that the testing
of your faith develops perseverance.

JAMES 1:2-3

TRIALS. TESTS. DIFFICULTIES. Struggles. Sources of frustration. We all have them. We all know the feelings that linger behind each: discouragement, defeat, and weariness.

I feel tried and tired by the relentless nature of my son's type I diabetes. I feel easily overwhelmed by the never-get-a-break nature of the disease. As with any condition that requires constant calculating and adjustments, I struggle with feeling defeated.

But I've come to realize that the Lord has a plan for my child and family that includes diabetes. That plan has involved meeting and ministering to other families that struggle with diabetes. Because we are confident in God's sovereignty in our situation, we can offer comfort to others. "So that we can comfort those in any trouble with the comfort we ourselves have received from God" (2 Cor. 1:4).

When we face trials of any kind, can we, like Paul, say, "I consider it pure joy"? Can we feel joy through our struggles as we are used to minister to others in Christ's name? Can we feel joy in knowing that the Lord considers us worthy of facing the challenge set before us? Not that we have to be martyrs—no one *likes* physical or emotional pain. But through our painful situations, God has a plan that will reflect His greatness.

The more difficult the challenge, the more we are being prepared to reflect God's magnificent abilities. I want to be part of whatever the Lord is doing—whatever will bring Him the most glory. Don't you also consider serving Him a privilege and an occasion for joy?

MORE SCRIPTURE FOR STUDY:
Ecclesiastes 7:14; Romans 5:1-5;
2 Corinthians 1:3-11; 1 Peter 3:15-16

Follow the Leader

*I took you from the pasture and from following the flock
to be ruler over my people.*

2 SAMUEL 7:8b

SHEEP CRAVE DIRECTION and the safety that boundaries offer. When left to their own inclinations, sheep will wander aimlessly, blithely eat poisonous plants, and fall into ditches. When David compared people to sheep in the Psalms (see Psalm 23), I've often hoped that he did so because we are easily led, not because we are stupid.

When the Lord called David to a leadership position in Israel, He used the above words from 2 Samuel. In essence the Lord was saying to David, "I want you to be a leader. You don't have to follow haplessly along with the other sheep." How did the Lord prepare David's mind for the job of leading a nation? By allowing him to be a shepherd to real sheep first. How did the Lord prepare David's heart for leading? By giving him a desire to follow God.

Lee Iacocca, the former president and chairman of the Chrysler Corporation, is credited with motivating people by saying, "Lead, follow, or get out of the way." He concisely summed up each personality trait known to mankind. We are either leaders, followers, or sit-by-the-side-of-the-roaders.

As Christians we're really both leaders and followers, aren't we? Like David, we have to know how to follow before we can lead well. Jesus' words to Peter were simply "Follow me" (John 21:19). In following Christ we learn how to lead, because He will always place people in our lives that need to be led. The Lord might call us to lead a small flock of our own children. We may be asked to lead as an example through modeling faith in our workplaces. He may want us to lead by serving on committees or teaching at church.

Jesus' words are also for us. He's called us out of the go-with-the-flow flock to lead. Will you follow David's example?

MORE SCRIPTURE FOR STUDY:
2 Chronicles 1:8-12; Proverbs 31:10-31;
Isaiah 40:11; Ezekiel 34; John 21:15-17

Silence

The LORD is in his holy temple; let all the earth be silent before him.

HABAKKUK 2:20

I'VE HEARD DEAFENING silence. That phrase seems to be an oxymoron. How can you *hear* the absence of sound? I have heard it in a snowstorm—not during a northeaster when you can hear the snowflakes crashing into each other, the wind howling, and feel the shaking trees. Rather, I hear silence in a steady, heavy snowfall. It "sounds" peacefully lazy as it cushions the ground, insulates the trees, and shelters the bushes and rocks. The silence builds with each inch of snow. All sounds are muffled. Yet the feeling of the silence echoes. That's what's deafening: the gigantic emptiness that we so desire to fill with noise.

During a deep snowfall I often reflect on the above verse from Habakkuk: "Let all the earth be silent before him." Cease our chattering. Stop our incessant need to be heard. Release our love affair with our own voices.

God's voice is the only voice of importance. Our self-centeredness, in voice and actions, ruins everything. Numbers 35:34 warns us: "Do not defile the land where you live and where I dwell, for I, the LORD, dwell among the Israelites." We "defile" His land with pollution of all kinds—noise being just one.

I think Habakkuk challenged the earth to be silent because we can form no sound, make no gesture, nor offer any action that can add to God's magnificence. It's as if the prophet was saying, "Chill out." In the Psalms we're told, "Be still and know that I am God" (Ps. 46:10a). This verse in effect reminds us to be quiet in God's presence. This isn't to say that we shouldn't offer our voices to the Lord and honor Him in songs and in praise. We sometimes just need to be quiet too.

If you live in a snow state, during the next snowstorm listen for the silence. (In states where snow is a no-show, find the quietest place you can—on a mountain, in the desert, or next to a lake.) Allow yourself to be drawn into the quiet and just be. "Let all the earth be silent before him."

MORE SCRIPTURE FOR STUDY:
Psalm 116:16; Matthew 25:14-30;
1 Corinthians 12

Sewing Lessons

No one tears a patch from a new garment and sews it on an old one.
If he does, he will have torn the new garment,
and the patch from the new will not match the old.

LUKE 5:36

ANTIQUE QUILTS PROVIDE a history of a family. Grandmother's calico apron becomes petals on a quilt with a floral design; pieces of the baby blanket shared by five children act as the stems of the floral pattern; and the old muslin curtains from the living room edge the entire quilt. A quilt tells a story of lives lived and seasons past. It brings something new and comforting from something old, worn out, and beyond repair.

I think of quilts and sewing when I read the above verse from Luke. And I'm not a sewer. I don't even *own* a sewing machine. But I can understand what Jesus communicated in these verses. How ludicrous it is to cut a piece of cloth from a brand-new article of clothing. It's like clipping a portion of my new fleece jacket and sewing it on my smelly barn coat. That would deface both of them. I might still wear the old barn coat, but the new fleece coat would be rendered useless (unless I want to walk around with a hole in my jacket).

How true in our lives. We're pretty attached to the "old" in our lives aren't we? Ripped and patched, holes and more patches—these "clothes" feel comfortable. They are the clothes of grief, depression, sadness, or anger. We shrug into them every day, determined to keep wearing them.

Romans 13:14 tells us to "clothe yourselves with the Lord Jesus Christ." We can believe this; yet while knowing that Jesus has forgiven us and given us new, bright, and crisp attire, we sometimes clip little pieces off the new and thread them on the old. Why? Because the threadbare attire is all we know. We feel comfortable wearing it.

We need to throw away the old and lay claim to 2 Corinthians 5:17: "If anyone is in Christ, he is a new creation; the old has gone, the new has come!" Make a commitment to the Lord to drop those old clothes right off your shoulders and slip on Christ's new garment for you. And throw away your tempting scissors!

MORE SCRIPTURE FOR STUDY:
Psalm 30:11-12; Luke 24:46-49;
Colossians 3:12-14; 1 Peter 5:4-10

The Lord Is Trustworthy

You are God! Your words are trustworthy.

2 SAMUEL 7:28

Multiplied Blessings

He answered, "You give them something to eat." They said to him,
"That would take eight months of a man's wages!"…
"How many loaves do you have?" he asked. "Go and see."
When they found out, they said, "Five—and two fish."

MARK 6:37-38

WHAT SEEMS IMPOSSIBLE to man is possible to the Lord—not only possible but easy. Such is the above story. Five loaves of bread and two fish were a ridiculously scant amount to feed a hungry crowd of over 5,000 (not counting the women and children) who had followed Jesus' boat offshore (Mark 6:33). But with Jesus around, there was enough to satisfy their hunger and leave twelve basketfuls of leftovers. That's a miracle of multiplication. There's no easy way to divide five loaves and two fish by 5,000 and get a remainder of twelve.

This miracle reminds me of how often we look at our full calendars and feel that we have nothing left to give. We feel as bare as a winter branch in New England. Tired and bent to the breaking point, we can feel our energy reserves begin to snap as we think of having two days of work to accomplish in twenty-four hours. We need a multiplication miracle of time—and that's just for the immediate needs at home!

Suppose you then get a call from a friend needing prayer or just a listening ear. Or, your child inconveniently gets sick, or a family member is in crisis. You're needed, but all you feel you can offer is a meager effort at best. Will you offer what you do have, ask for God's blessing, and then submit your willingness in faith that your effort will be used for His purposes? When you respond to someone else's need with a willing heart, the Lord is faithful not only to fulfill the need but also to multiply the blessing. The other person feels blessed, and you'll find yourself blessed by God's sustenance for both of you.

In the coming weeks when an unplanned call or situation diverts your attention and saps your time and energy, remember what Jesus did when faced with the hungry crowd. "Taking the five loaves and the two fish and looking up to heaven, he gave thanks and broke the loaves. Then he gave them to his disciples to set before the people.... They all ate and were satisfied" (Mark 6:41-42).

MORE SCRIPTURE FOR STUDY:
Psalm 103:1-5; Matthew 10:6-8; Luke 6:38; John 12:24-26

Daily Victory

Everything exposed by the light becomes visible, for it is light that makes everything visible.

EPHESIANS 5:13-14a

I AWOKE WITH THE WORDS, *Take joy in the morning,* edging the rim of my consciousness. But I felt too lethargic to let the words take hold of my heart. The day ahead was littered with commitments, a pesky argument with Peter weighted my mood, and I knew I needed to apologize to a friend about something I had said.

I went outside in the early morning to take a brisk, wake-up walk on the hard-packed, dirt road. After what seemed like an endless week of gray clouds and snow showers, the pale sun crested the eastern sky. I watched it creep up, pushing long shadows ahead of it across the road. *Take joy in the morning* slipped into my mind again. I felt so grateful to see the sun that I nearly cried. I hadn't known how much I had missed it during the past week.

As the sun's rays grew stronger, I could understand why I had been impressed with the words, *Take joy in the morning.* I remembered that just a few days before I had told my son about the parallel between Jesus as the center of our lives and the sun as the center of our solar system. The sun is a reflection of the Son. A light went on in his head that day and finally penetrated my heart during my early morning walk days later.

The sun, lighting my way as my pace quickened, reminded me yet again of the Lord's promise that light would always overtake darkness. It assured me of Jesus' victory over sin.

Second Peter talks of light removing darkness in our souls: "Until the day dawns and the morning star rises in your hearts" (1:19). The morning star is Christ, who pushes the darkness of sin away from us and reveals His glory in its stead.

Each new day the sun rises without fail and on time.

Each new day reminds us of God's faithfulness as His light overtakes the darkness.

Each new day refreshes our souls as our sins are taken away with the dismissal of darkness.

I'll take joy in that kind of morning each new day!

MORE SCRIPTURE FOR STUDY:
Psalms 5:1-3, 11-12; 16:8-11;
Lamentations 3:19-24; 1 John 5:4-5

Landmarks

*This stone that I have set up as a pillar
will be God's house.*

GENESIS 28:22

NUMEROUS SNOWFALLS HIDE the usual landmarks on the trails around
our home. During the summer I ride horseback on those trails; in the winter I
ski on them. With the trees stripped of foliage the woods open up into decep-
tively same-looking branches of gray and brown. The worn footpath, mud-
died with use in the summer, is hidden under the uniform white. The area looks
as though tributary trails lead off in each direction, even though I know there
aren't any. A landmark downed tree where I usually bear right looks innocent
blanketed with white. The snow hides the jagged edges I scoot around on horseback in the summer.

Yet seeing the landmarks, even as different as they look in the winter, offers
me comfort. Why do we need landmarks? These well-known markers tell us
where we are. We feel a whisper of relief, knowing we're on track. Landmarks
confirm that we are safely heading toward our intended destination.

Jacob's well was a landmark for Jesus and the disciples in John 4. We know this story as the one in which the Samaritan woman came to the saving knowledge of Jesus. But the well was also a marker. Historically it marked Joseph's inheritance from his father Jacob. It also was a source of water for the people of Sychar. Ultimately, this landmark was the place preordained for Jesus to meet the Samaritan woman. The fact that Jacob's well was the place set aside for this life-changing meeting wasn't accidental. Rather, it was part of God's plan to include non-Jewish people in this message of hope. This living water was for all.

The Lord puts strategic landmarks in our lives—people, events, or places—to remind us of His presence and the security of being in His will. Will you recognize the markers He sets out as they offer you the assurance of His path for you?

MORE SCRIPTURE FOR STUDY:
Exodus 24:1-4; Joshua 4:1-9; 14:9;
Proverbs 3:5-6; John 4:1-42

Willing to Be Used

Put out into deep water, and let down the nets for a catch.

LUKE 5:4

FEBRUARY OFTEN HAS chilling rainfalls. When the temperature hovers above freezing, the rain either turns the snow to heavy slush or creates a layer of ice on it. Mini-glaciers form from the layers of ice in the streams and brooks. Sometimes water works its way through the ice, sending rivers under the ice cap and into the streambeds.

On an otherwise quiet day, while standing on the deck of our home, I can hear the rush of water from the stream in the valley below the house as the water cascades over the top of the ice. A duller roar can be heard underneath. Later in the spring when I investigate the brook with the children, we find sediment built up along the stream edges, stones polished, and the land around the stream raw from the overflow.

Water in its natural downhill course can cause damage. It washes away loose debris. What's left? Only the solid foundation of the riverbed, the heaviest rocks, and the trees with the deepest root structures.

In the river of God's plan, I would choose to be a rock solidly placed in the middle of the riverbed—a rock that helps change the course of the stream of others' lives. The water's wearing at my sharp edges, smoothing the points to a fine polish would be welcome. I would want my base to be solid and used as a sturdy stepping stone. The purifying process of the water flowing over, under, and around me would be appreciated.

Would you also want to be a rock in the stream? Maybe you would prefer to see yourself as a small stone, willingly carried along in God's stream as He directs your course. Or, maybe you'd rather be one of many pebbles pushed along. When joined with others, you form a stream-spanning bridge of dry ground.

Each of these options displays our differences; yet all are beneficial when we are willing to "go with the flow" of how the Lord wants to use us in His river. Will you pray with me?

Rain on me, Lord.
Let Your water carry me where I can be the most useful.

MORE SCRIPTURE FOR STUDY:
1 Chronicles 28:7-10; Proverbs 2:7-8, 20-22;
Ephesians 4:29-32; 2 Timothy 2:21

A Common Language

The LORD God had formed out of the ground all the beasts....
He brought them to the man to see what he would name
them.... So the man gave names to all the livestock,
the birds of the air and all the beasts of the field.

GENESIS 2:19-20

I ENJOY NAMING each new child or pet that joins our family (except our chickens). Our children and each young animal we've had the fun of naming have been christened after a place to which Peter or I have traveled. Hence Geneva and Jordan (our children); Galilee (my horse); Gibraltar and Tupper Lake (the dogs); Lincoln, Scotland, and Squam Lake (the cats). You get the idea.

When I read about Adam having the privilege of naming the animals in Genesis 2, I like to think he enjoyed the task. But think on that for a minute. What's needed to name anything? Language. Adam had been created already knowing a language that became the universal language until the tower of Babel (Gen.11:1-9).

There are literally thousands of languages and dialect variations now; yet a common language still exists. It crosses all boundaries, all cultures, all ages. The language is in God's created nature. "The heavens declare the glory of God; the skies proclaim the work of his hands. Day after day they pour forth speech; night after night they display knowledge. *There is no speech or language where their voice is not heard*" (Ps.19:1-3—italics added).

God's universal language through His creation is for everyone's benefit. It is a unifier for all people. Anyone, regardless of tongue, can grasp the concepts of light versus darkness; good versus evil; growth versus destruction. Each represents the Lord's sovereignty over death. This common dialect even reaches those who have a severe mental impairment or limited language ability. They can still experience the feelings attached to good versus evil.

Look around you this winter and see—really see—God's language through His creation. What examples of His victory over darkness and death can you find in His display of nature?

MORE SCRIPTURE FOR STUDY:
Deuteronomy 30:19-20; Job 37; Psalm 89:48

Growing Up

When I was a child, I talked like a child, I thought like a child,
I reasoned like a child. When I became a man,
I put childish ways behind me.

1 CORINTHIANS 13:11

WHILE I WAS IN MY TWENTIES, I could abuse my body with poor nutrition, lack of exercise (or too much exercise without a proper warm-up), and not enough sleep. I rebounded easily with few consequences. I could function for two or three days on a total of twelve hours of sleep. I never gained an ounce despite eating high-fat foods. But when I hit my early thirties, my metabolism changed. I felt tired more easily and needed an afternoon nap to make it through dinner. My body ached if I didn't take care in exercising. And—what's worse—I started gaining weight.

I had to face it: I couldn't "get away" with nonchalant care of myself anymore. Does that sound familiar?

Simultaneously, I noticed the Lord working in my spirit. I couldn't "get away" with a haphazard approach to my relationship with Him. As He called me into a deeper communion with Him, I began to feel uncomfortable with my previous approach of "catch-up-with-You-when-I-can, Lord."

He started to hold me accountable for my attitudes or opinions of others. The Holy Spirit convicted me about my quick, hurtful tongue. I had a lot of growing up to do! Don't we all?

Paul talks about "growing up" in the above verse. Have you too felt the Lord drawing you out of your adolescent ways? Is He calling you to a maturity where you just can't "get away" with certain responses or attitudes anymore? Paul chastens those living spiritually immature lives: "You need milk, not solid food! Anyone who lives on milk … is not acquainted with the teaching about righteousness. But solid food is for the mature" (Heb. 5:12-14).

Will you pray with me?

Lord, give me a taste for Your solid food
so that I can leave behind my childish ways.

MORE SCRIPTURE FOR STUDY:
Psalm 51:6; 1 Corinthians 3:1-3;
Ephesians 4:12-16; Colossians 1:10-12

Shelter

My people will live in peaceful dwelling places,
in secure homes, in undisturbed places of rest.

ISAIAH 32:18

SNOW HAD FALLEN during the night, deep enough to cover the worn, crusty layer that had been fluffy just a few weeks before. It was a perfect morning for cross-country skiing—bright sun, puffy clouds, and cold enough to keep the snow powdery.

My family and I set off on skis down the familiar trail. Feeling adventurous, we decided to cross a valley, intending to arrive at a field on the other side. Making our way downhill to the base of the valley, we came across a deer "yard." Sheltered under thick hemlock branches and facing south, the yard looked to be the home of several deer. The area around the base of the trees was trampled, droppings littered the area, and worn narrow paths led away from the refuge. Munched twigs and rub marks on the trees told the story of a family that spent a great deal of time there, protected overhead by the canopy of evergreens. We could imagine them lying warm flank to warm flank, chewing their cud, waiting for the winter storms to pass. I felt God's impression: *They are as secure and content in the shelter of My hand as you are.*

"He who dwells in the shelter of the Most High will rest in the shadow of the Almighty. I will say of the LORD, 'He is my refuge and my fortress, my God, in whom I trust.' … Under his wings you will find refuge" (Psalm 91:1-4a).

Can you imagine how it must please our heavenly Father when we feel safe in His protection? When the icy winds of fear threaten us, can we remember to honor Him with our trust? His tender and eternal promises and His very character form the protective canopy over our heads—the protection under which we can rest securely.

MORE SCRIPTURE FOR STUDY:
Psalms 63:2-8; 131; Hebrews 4

Endpoints

It was you who set all the boundaries of the earth;
you made both summer and winter.

PSALM 74:17

TOWARD THE END of February I'm ready for a change in weather. The air feels old and rain comes nearly as much as the snow. The worst part is that I know we probably still have at least six more weeks of wet and cold weather. (It snowed once on Mother's Day. That was disheartening!)

One day I came across the above verse and suddenly felt profoundly grateful for the seasons—even if I was sick of the current one. What did the psalmist mean by the words "set all the boundaries"? He meant that there is an *end* to everything on earth. Everything has a clearly defined, predetermined stopping point. What did that mean to me in the midst of my winter doldrums? Winter (and all of the seasons) would end because of the boundaries God established at the beginning of creation.

For what else do many of us impatiently seek an end? Sickness, pregnancy, two-year-old tantrums, a lousy job, incarceration, school, even our very lives at times. We anxiously await the imagined "time's up!" cry.

I wonder if this might have been what Solomon was thinking when he wrote the "time for everything" passage in Ecclesiastes 3:1-8. Maybe his thoughts weren't so much in anticipation of the various "seasons" of life but rather the assured ending of each unpleasant circumstance.

There has to be an ending in order for a new beginning to occur, doesn't there? Is there something you are waiting to see come to an end? Are you awaiting a new beginning? If a boundary is indeed an endpoint, can you echo the psalmist's words as you consider the seasons of your life? Will you trust our everlasting Father that the endpoint He has in mind for your current season is indeed coming in His timing?

MORE SCRIPTURE FOR STUDY:
Job 26:7-14; Psalms 90:1-4; 93;
Ecclesiastes 3:1-14

Impressions

I bear on my body the marks of Jesus.

GALATIANS 6:17

PETER POURED THE CONCRETE SLAB upon which our barn was built in the summer of 1986. Between the time of pouring the soupy concrete and its setting, Peter and I pressed our right hands into the concrete on the southern edge of the slab. I remember the feel of it oozing between my fingers. I determinedly pushed down even harder, wanting to be sure my imprint could be seen and would last. With a stick I etched the date next to our prints.

Horses came and went in the barn. Two children were born. I forgot about the prints until one winter day when I found then four-year-old Jordan kneeling on the southern threshold, placing his mittened hand on the concrete floor, then lifting it up again to look underneath. He'd found our handprints. He took his mitten off and spread his fingers wide to fit into his daddy's print. But his fingers were too short and too narrow to fit the spot. He pulled his mitten back on, stood up, shrugged, and wandered off.

It made me think about the impression Peter and I are leaving for our children. Will they be able to fit into the impressions we've set for them? Will they even want to try to fill our prints? Will they desire to press in to the Lord as we've tried to model for them?

Any interaction with the Lord as our Savior leaves a visible impression on our lives. Jesus in our hearts leaves a mark of ownership. Exodus 21:6 talks of the mark of ownership: "His master must take him before the judges. He shall take him to the door or the doorpost and pierce his ear with an awl. Then he will be his servant for life."

As a servant of the Lord, I want there to be a print on me from where I've pressed in to Him. I want to leave a deep and penetrating impression for my children, not a shallow, barely noticeable mark. Will you pray with me?

Pierce my ear, Lord.
Let Your mark of ownership
be a discernible impression for others.

MORE SCRIPTURE FOR STUDY:
Deuteronomy 6:4-9; Psalm 40:5-10;
2 Corinthians 1:21-22; Philippians 3:12-21

Beauty in the Eye of the Beholder

He has made everything beautiful in its time.

ECCLESIASTES 3:11a

FROM WHERE DO WE GET our taste for beauty? And what exactly determines what we find attractive? I like a new snowfall, fresh in its whiteness. That's beautiful to me. Conversely, I don't like old, brown, gritty snow. That's ugly to me. Most would agree with me about both of those thoughts.

But what about other things? What about giving birth, people with disfigurements, or an overgrown garden? Can we see beauty beyond the visuals? Can we see God's creative hand amidst pain, brokenness, or disarray?

In Eden everything was beautiful. There was no destruction or ugliness. Ugliness came into being when Adam and Eve's eyes were "opened" (Gen. 3:7). They became critical. Ugliness is based on a critical spirit. "That's not pretty," we might think. "How disgusting," we might say as we avert our eyes.

But 1 Corinthians 14:33 says, "God is not a God of disorder, but of peace." Can we take this to mean that whatever we think is ugly or unsightly could be part of God's orderly plan? A measure of God's order is to bring glory to Himself, especially in the face of our limited perceptions of beauty.

"He has made everything beautiful in its time" is preceded by Solomon's discourse on a time for everything (Eccl. 3:1-8). In each of the "seasons" he suggests a proactive stance and, conversely, a relinquishing attitude. I believe the beauty he speaks of two verses later comes in releasing all of our presumptions to the Lord. When we do, He can take something unsightly and turn it into something beautiful for His glory. Each of the "ugly" scenarios will turn into something profitable for Him.

I desire to see beauty with the Lord's eyes. Will you pray with me?

Lord, open my eyes to Your plan of order and peace.
Let my eyes see the beauty You have in mind
for everything I see.

MORE SCRIPTURE FOR STUDY:
Psalm 119:18; Isaiah 61:1-3; Malachi 4:2;
Romans 8:18-21, 28

Rock Solid

See, I lay a stone in Zion, a tested stone, a precious cornerstone
for a sure foundation; the one who trusts
will never be dismayed.

ISAIAH 28:16

OUR PROPERTY LIES along the edge of what used to be a several-hundred-acre parcel of land known as the Page Estate. The land is divided now between several families. Yet the old stone foundations on our neighbor's property tell the story of huge barns, square houses, and even old gardens that are now overrun with forsythia, day lilies, and myrtle in the spring and summer. Close to 200 years old, the foundations only hint at the buildings they once supported. Their wood frames have long ago rotted into the ground. Yet the stone cellars stand solid, firmly keeping the earth from caving in.

My children and I like to explore what they call "the ruins" and speculate on what the houses and barns looked like and how the people lived. We always seem to be drawn to the granite rock walls. We suspect that oxen dragged the fieldstones to the building site, pulleys and levers hoisted the rocks to the right spot, and men strong-armed each rock into place. I also know they paid very careful attention to the very first boulder they maneuvered into place. Why? That first rock would determine the squareness of the rest of the foundation. The entire dwelling's strength and security rested on that cornerstone. The first stone was the measure by which all else could be established.

Likewise, Jesus is our cornerstone. "You are no longer foreigners and aliens, but fellow citizens with God's people and members of God's household … with Christ Jesus himself as the chief cornerstone. In him the whole building is joined together and rises to become a holy temple in the Lord" (Eph. 2:19-21). Without the solid, straight-edged base of Christ we cannot have a secure building. Psalm 127:1 says, "Unless the LORD builds the house, its builders labor in vain."

Don't you want to live in the house our Lord built, the house where Jesus Himself is the cornerstone of eternity?

MORE SCRIPTURE FOR STUDY:
Isaiah 26:4; Zechariah 10:4;
Matthew 7:24-29; 1 Peter 2:4-12

Give Credit

These are but the outer fringe of his works; how faint the whisper we hear of him!

JOB 26:14a

THE VERSE ABOVE is one of my most treasured verses of the Bible. It speaks so eloquently of all I want to say about how small we are and how immeasurably great the Lord is. There is so much more to the Lord than what we can see, understand, or hope to communicate. We can only understand a fraction of how awesome He is.

Yet the Lord calls us to praise Him for His works. "Ascribe to the LORD, O families of nations, ascribe to the LORD glory and strength, ascribe to the LORD the glory due his name" (1 Chron. 16:28-29a). Why are we instructed to "ascribe" (give due credit) to the Lord? He certainly doesn't need our edification. He is all-powerful and doesn't need a constant affirmation of His greatness. (That is a human need!)

The reason we are repeatedly encouraged to praise Him—especially by David and other psalmists—is for our own benefit. Praising God helps us to see beyond ourselves and begin to understand our diminutive place in God's very big universe. I like the way the psalmist proclaims, "How good it is to sing praises to our God, how pleasant and fitting to praise him!" (Ps. 147:1).

What's amazing is that we each have a place and a purpose preordained by the Lord. His plan for us is another good reason to praise Him, isn't it? We don't need to fret, because God has everything under control. "No eye has seen, no ear has heard, no mind has conceived what God has prepared for those who love him" (1 Cor. 2:9).

Will you add your voice of praise in the hope that "the whole earth be filled with his glory" (Ps. 72:19)?

MORE SCRIPTURE FOR STUDY:
Psalms 8; 148; 1 Corinthians 10:31

The Lord Is Faithful

O LORD, you are my God; I will exalt you and praise your name,
for in perfect faithfulness you have done marvelous things,
things planned long ago.

ISAIAH 25:1

Enough to Spare

Give, and it will be given to you. A good measure, pressed down,
shaken together and running over, will be poured into your lap.
For with the measure you use, it will be measured to you.

LUKE 6:38

LATE WINTER/EARLY SPRING marks the run of sap in the sugar maples across New England. Sugarin' season starts when the nights still send fingers of frost, but the daytime sun warms the ground enough to release water.

Maple sugar farmers hammer metal spouts into the trees. The clear, semi-sweet liquid then drips into buckets or trickles down tubing into a giant tank. Truck, tractor, and sometimes snowmobile or horses are used to transport the sap to the sugarhouse. The sap boils in giant vats for hours until it thickens and darkens at the maple syrup stage. It takes about forty gallons of sap to make one gallon of syrup.

The water that becomes sap is dormant underground until it flows upward, bringing life-giving nourishment to the branches. So the question is asked, "Doesn't tapping the trees for sap hurt them in some way? Doesn't it deprive them of necessary food? Doesn't it stunt their growth?" No. Sugar maples have sap to spare.

When I think of the life-giving lesson of the sap, I can't help but think of myself. How often do I want to hang on to what has nourished me, not willing to pass it on to others? Am I willing to share the blessings that the Lord has given me: my home, finances, or time? I'm learning that there's always enough to spare. The Lord always replaces what He's asked me to give.

Will you allow the Lord to "tap" you for the life-giving abundance He's given you?

MORE SCRIPTURE FOR STUDY:
Psalm 132:15; Matthew 13:12; 25:14-30;
1 Peter 4:9-11

Walls of Protection

The boundary lines have fallen for me in pleasant places.

PSALM 16:6a

STONE WALL BOUNDARIES edge farms across New England. Deeds read, *Follow stone wall north for 93 steps to intersect with northwest stone wall.* These rock walls—literally 200-300 years old—act as dividers of pastures, markers for property lines, and fences along old travel routes.

It's been said that building a stone wall was a two-season process. During the spring months of plowing and planting, handpicked rocks were piled along the edges of the fields. Oxen or horses dragged the bigger boulders. In late fall the men worked to build the stone walls before the deep snow arrived. The biggest rocks formed two parallel lines about two feet apart, while the smaller rocks filled in the center between the rows.

I've noticed that the Lord uses a two-step, boundary-laying process with us as we draw closer to Him. First, He has to uncover, weed out, and clear away the "rocks" in our lives. Some of our rocks have the sharp edges of defiance, rebellion, anger, pride, etc.

Second, after the season of harvesting rocks passes, the Lord uses what

He's removed from us to form barriers for us. These are tender walls of protection. Within the "pleasant places" we are free to graze, roam, and be fed. There are no rocky points of greed or idolatry to trip us. Yet the lines of safety are clearly defined. If we get too close to the rocks He's removed from us, we may stumble and take a hard fall back into rebellion or deceit. The boundary walls serve to remind us, "Don't go there."

This season, pray about the rocks that the Lord may be prying out of your spirit. Document the rocks, pebbles, and boulders He removes. Use them as boundaries to stay away from in the coming seasons.

MORE SCRIPTURE FOR STUDY:
Psalms 19:7-13; 51:1-10; Proverbs 12:1;
Acts 3:19; 2 Peter 3:9

Swept Clean

He lifted me out of the slimy pit, out of the mud and mire.

PSALM 40:2a

Many people from the southern states or the Midwest laugh at the idea of mudrooms in New England houses. But mudrooms are a standard part of New England home construction. Mudrooms are used for ... well ... mud.

Many rural communities in the Northeast are situated on dirt roads. Some towns in the northern parts of Maine, Vermont, and New Hampshire have a greater number of dirt roads than paved roads. Though the roads are scenic and have a "natural" feel, they turn to mud during the spring thaw and rains. Mud gets caked on everything—hence the need for mudrooms. We kick off our oozing shoes and sweep the mudroom several times a day.

The point of the mudroom, of course, is to minimize the tracking of dirt into the house. Wouldn't it be nice if we could confine the mud of our lives to just one "room" in our souls too? There the dirt would stay to be swept up before it dirtied every other room in our lives. But the problem with our human nature is that our dirt follows us from place to place leaving a gritty residue behind.

Aren't you grateful that we have a faithful and generous Housecleaner? Our Lord sweeps up our dirt and throws it in the trash bin. That doesn't give us leave to keep tracking dirt into our souls. It does mean we can get a fresh start when we sincerely ask the Lord to sweep out our mudrooms.

"Let us draw near to God with a sincere heart in full assurance of faith, having our hearts sprinkled to cleanse us" (Heb. 10:22). Pray with me:

Lord, thank You
that You are the Master cleaner of my mudroom.
Let me be willing to hand You the broom to start sweeping.

MORE SCRIPTURE FOR STUDY:
Isaiah 1:18; 56:7; Matthew 23:25-26;
1 Peter 2:5

Paying Attention

Foxes have holes and birds of the air have nests.

MATTHEW 8:20

AS I EMPTIED the wheelbarrow of the day's gatherings from the horse stalls, I looked out across the valley to the next hillside. There I saw what looked like a scruffy orange-brown dog. Against the wet snow I could see the animal sit up, turn a few circles, and lie down—all very doglike activities. I trotted to the house and returned to the edge of the barnyard with a pair of binoculars. As soon as I focused on the animal I saw that it was a red fox. Beyond where she was curled I could see brown dirt and a dark hole—the entrance to her den.

When I whistled, her head shot up and her ears pricked forward on the alert. Her nostrils flared to take in my smell.

Over the next several weeks the patch of brown dirt widened around the entrance to her den. She was digging deep. Each day I would whistle to her from the edge of the barnyard. She would come out of the den and answer silently by staring back at me.

A few weeks passed when I didn't see her. Finally, she reappeared with five tiny scruff balls scampering at her feet. They fascinated me. Each day I would watch them venture farther and farther from their home. They played, yapped, and chased each other while their mother watched quietly. One day they simply disappeared. For a few days I called, but I never saw them again. I felt sad—my little fox family had moved on.

I learned a lesson about myself from my interchange with the little family. I suddenly felt keenly aware of and embarrassed by the transient nature of my relationship with people. Why is it that I could stare in wonder at the Lord's creation of my mama fox friend, but ignore my human friend's new baby? If I put as much effort into caring for God's people as I put into watching the fox family, maybe I could affect lives more! How often have I not taken an opportunity to touch someone's life through a kind word or gesture?

How about you? Do you respond with compassion or impatience in the brief interchanges with the people around you? This week try to see each person with whom you come in contact as someone who deserves a few minutes of your undivided attention.

MORE SCRIPTURE FOR STUDY:
Isaiah 61:1-3; Matthew 9:35-38;
Philippians 2:1-4; 1 Peter 2:9-10

New Hope

*Let us throw off everything that hinders and the sin
that so easily entangles.*

HEBREWS 12:1b

A CERTAIN SIGN OF SPRING is the musty odor underfoot from the leaves that blew down after the last fall raking. The brown leaves collected every possible drop of moisture from the winter snows.

On the first warm day Peter and I start gathering the leftover leaves. Unraked leaves turn into a science project of mold, mildew, and slime. Since the leaves are heavy with water and stick to each other, maneuvering them takes strong arms and backs. Sometimes we'll comment to one another, "Why are we bothering to do this? It's hard work!" Our answer is echoed by anyone who rakes leaves in his or her yard. Allowing the leaves to stay makes the lawn look unkempt. Removing the leaves allows the sun to nurture the new grass.

Don't you find that once the new growth pops up—sometimes as quickly as within a few days—the raking seems worth the effort? As a matter of fact, we expect to see new growth after getting rid of the leaves. It's an unspoken promise of hope.

Yet why do we sometimes lack that same expectancy in our faith walks? Why do we muddle through each day disheartened by the same dead leaves of mistakes and attitudes? Do we think that the effort of removing the brown muck in our lives is too much? Do we really *believe* that new growth is right under the surface just waiting to be uncovered? Do we have a confident *hope* in what's underneath?

Philippians 1:20a says, "I eagerly expect and hope that I will in no way be ashamed, but will have sufficient courage." Do you have the courage to rake up the dead leaves in your life? Do you expect to see new growth? Near the end of Romans 8, Paul concludes that "seen" hope is not really hope (i.e., that's a cheater's hope). Instead we ought to hope for what we do not see (Romans 8:24-25).

Shall we start raking?

MORE SCRIPTURE FOR STUDY:
Psalm 25:3-5; Romans 15:13;
Philippians 3:12-14; 1 John 1:5-10

Bent but Not Broken

*A bruised reed he will not break, and a smoldering wick
he will not snuff out.*

ISAIAH 42:3a

A SMALL THATCH OF CATTAILS grows in a marshy area along the road edge of our property. I've watched their slow growth and multiplication, always anticipating that "next year" I'll be able to cut a few to dry and use in a floral arrangement.

One spring day a small truck pulled into the marshy spot where the cattails grew. Its tires spun and eventually edged out. But the tires left some of the stalks completely broken off and others precariously bent. I felt angry that my little group had been disturbed and broken. Plus I had to wait until the fall to see if they would recover.

Watching the few cattails struggle to recuperate from the invasion of the truck gave me the imagery of the above verse from Isaiah: "A bruised reed he will not break." Haven't we also had run-ins with trouble that left us feeling bruised and battered?

I know how a "bruised reed" feels—downtrodden, weak, and discouraged. I feel walked-over when someone takes advantage of me. I feel weak when a relationship isn't working the way that I had hoped. I feel discouraged when expectations go unmet. How about you?

But the verse from Isaiah reminds us that the Lord will not break us when we are downcast. He may allow us to stay bent for a time. He may allow us to come to the brink of feeling severed. Why? Hope in Him and His healing strength keeps us from being permanently broken. He also gives us this promise: "The Lord is close to the brokenhearted and saves those who are crushed in spirit" (Ps. 34:18).

When you feel bent and bruised, consider reading the book of Job for a graphic description of a "bruised reed." Take special note of the last verses of the last chapter: "The LORD blessed the latter part of Job's life more than the first.... After this, Job lived a hundred and forty years; he saw his children and their children to the fourth generation" (Job 42:12-16).

We can find a lot of hope in those words. We too will not be broken. Instead the Lord will heal our bruises and straighten our bent stalks.

MORE SCRIPTURE FOR STUDY:
Psalm 42:5-11; Isaiah 30:26;
Matthew 12:15-21; Hebrews 10:22-23

Where Is Your Focus?

I lift up my eyes to the hills—where does my help come from?
My help comes from the LORD, the Maker of
heaven and earth.

PSALM 121:1-2

A FRIEND OF OURS hiked the entire Appalachian Trail a couple of years ago. Beginning in March in Georgia, he hiked the approximate 2,150 miles to finish in October on the top of Mount Katahdin in Maine. Clambering over mountains, sometimes two or three a day, I assumed he must have marveled at God's beautiful creation. But his comments surprised me: "When you're hiking the Trail, you spend about 90 percent of your time looking at your feet and the path right in front of you. If you don't, you'll fall flat on your face. Constantly looking down makes your neck ache and your shoulders burn. But if you look around for more than a moment, you'll fall."

I found myself thinking about how his comments rang true in my walks too. While riding my horse through the woods, I find myself critically eyeing the next few footfalls. I cautiously step over downed trees and take a tentative hop across a mud hole. The only time I really look at the scene around me is when I stop. At that point I can feast on the canopy of new green growth over my head. I can see chipmunks chasing each other over a stone wall.

As the psalmist said, "I lift up my eyes to the hills." What does that mean? Stop looking down. In what ways do we look "down" in our spirits? Maybe we do so when we have a self-pitying or self-focused attitude. But when we look up and take the focus off our selves, what do we see? We see God's splendor around us. Listen to the rest of the psalmist's thoughts: "Where does my help come from?" (Take the focus off of self.) "My help comes from the LORD, the Maker of heaven and earth." (Look up for help, not down at self.) "He will not let your foot slip" (v. 3).

Stop and look all around you. Where is your focus—on your feet or on the Lord?

MORE SCRIPTURE FOR STUDY:
Psalm 141:8; Ephesians 1:18;
Colossians 3:1-3; Hebrews 12:2

Tread Gently

*They trample on the heads of the poor as upon
the dust of the ground.*

AMOS 2:7a

I HURT A DEAR FRIEND'S FEELINGS. My sharp tongue and cutting wit knocked my friend to her knees. I lashed at her with unkind words. But I didn't stop there. I proceeded to do a tap-dance on her spirit while she was down.

I am profoundly ashamed of these things. So why am I sharing this? Two reasons. One: I know I'm not alone in carrying anger too far sometimes. Two: the Lord in His humor and sovereignty allowed me to feel the physical sensation of what I had done to my friend emotionally.

A few days after I hurt my friend's feelings, my horse, Galilee, escaped from his paddock. He had felt unhappy outside by himself, so he freed himself and ran into the barn to be with the other horses. I caught him easily enough and led him back to his paddock. He was not amused. He *wanted* to be with his friends. (Need I say that horses are herd animals?) With a precision that I can only say was deliberate, he stepped his 1,200 pounds squarely on my foot, twisted his hoof across the top of my foot, crashed his shoulder into mine, and knocked me backward. He got his way and I got a broken foot.

As I hobbled around for the next several weeks, I recognized the parallel between being the trampler and the tramplee. Although I don't think I acted quite as deliberately toward my friend as my horse had toward me, the knocking down, trampling, and running over seemed pretty close.

Don't you find that the Lord uses an object lesson sometimes to show us our errors? I think He does this at times because we are so thickheaded that He has to physically shake us up a bit to get our attention.

The way to prevent an injury before exercising is to be more cautious: warm up and stretch first; go easy and slow. The same can be said in relationships: speak carefully with well-thought-out words. "Everyone should be quick to listen, slow to speak and slow to become angry" (James 1:19). If anger sometimes rules your tongue, will you repent of your tendency to trample and ask the Lord to give you a kinder mouth? In my case I might have spared myself some physical pain!

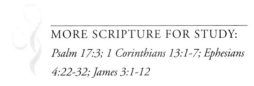

MORE SCRIPTURE FOR STUDY:
Psalm 17:3; 1 Corinthians 13:1-7; Ephesians 4:22-32; James 3:1-12

A Closet of New Clothes

Therefore, as God's chosen people, holy and dearly loved,
clothe yourselves with compassion, kindness,
humility, gentleness and patience.

COLOSSIANS 3:12

THOUGH SOLID IN STATURE, 200-year-old New England houses are missing one significant feature: closets. In truly old homes that have had few modifications, the rooms include four straight walls (with an occasional small window breaking up the space) but no doors, hidden vanities, shelves, or clothing racks. This is particularly true in Shaker communal homes where there simply wasn't a need for closets. They only owned two sets of clothes—what they wore on their backs and their church clothes. What they weren't wearing hung on a peg rack on the wall rather than in closets.

We can't imagine living in the twenty-first century without closets, can we? Yet that's exactly what we do in our spiritual lives. We haven't built or provided the space in our hearts for the clothes Christ gives us to wear. What clothes? Read the above verse again: compassion, kindness, humility, gentleness, and patience.

What do these "clothes" look like on our frames? A handkerchief of compassion to dry a friend's tears. A shirt of kindness to drape across your children's shoulders. The pants of humility worn at the knees from praying. Lamb's wool gloves of gentleness when communicating with your spouse. A coat of patience when you're laboring with your coworkers.

Do you have a big enough closet for the clothes that the Lord has for you? Maybe you need to do some renovations in your heart to build a closet to hold these treasured garments. Be sure to try them on and wear them with grace and dignity.

MORE SCRIPTURE FOR STUDY:
Deuteronomy 4:9; Joshua 22:5;
1 Samuel 10:6-7; Ezekiel 36:25-27;
Ephesians 4:22-24

The Telling Eyes

Be sure you know the conditions of your flocks,
give careful attention to your herds.

PROVERBS 27:23

A SHEPHERD KNOWS his sheep intimately. A person who spends a lot of time with animals (cattle rancher, horse trainer, dog breeder, etc.) learns to "read" the animal's behavior for any signs of distress, illness, or injury. (Sounds like a mother of children, too, doesn't it?)

Like other animal handlers, I use the look in an animal's eye to determine its mental and physical well-being. On three occasions I've seen "the look"—a dullness of eye—when the animal communicates, "I've had enough. I've served you well. Let me go." That doesn't make the decision to put an animal to sleep any easier; yet an animal's eyes don't lie. They know when it's time to go.

It's been said that the eye is the window to the soul. That's true in both animals and humans. In people we can see the reflection of physical pain in the wrinkles around the eyes. We can see emotional pain by the defeated, lethargic look in someone's eyes.

The above Proverb admonishes us to "know the condition of [our] flocks." Of whom are our "flocks" composed? Any person we are responsible for: our children, spouse, ministry coworkers, extended family—basically anybody we lead or over whom we have an influence. How can we "know" his or her condition? The eyes.

Look into the person's eyes as you talk with him or her. Ask her how she's doing and mean it. Get to know him through reading his eyes and facial expressions. Pray for discernment to read the nuances of the "flock" the Lord has entrusted to you.

MORE SCRIPTURE FOR STUDY:
1 Kings 3:9; Proverbs 20:5; 27:18-19;
Matthew 6:22-23; John 21:15-17

Debts Forgiven

For God so loved the world that he gave his one and only Son,
that whoever believes in him shall not perish
but have eternal life.

JOHN 3:16

I'VE LEARNED THAT as spring rolls around, I have a need to nurture something—anything. In part this is because my children were born in the middle to late winter. Most of our pets came to us in late winter or early spring. Plus, I'm a nurturer by nature. I desire to see things grow and develop.

That's why I love spring. It holds so much promise—the promise of nurturing new life. There's also the promise of not looking back but forward. I know what is past can no longer affect me unless I choose to allow it to. Through the forgiveness of Christ, poor choices are forgotten, wrongs are forgiven.

I'm reminded of the Year of Jubilee described in Leviticus 25:8-55. (See also Deuteronomy 15:1-11.) In Israel the Year of Jubilee was every seventh year. This was the year in which all debts were cancelled.

We don't have to wait for each seventh year for our debts to be cancelled.

Jesus took our debts—our shameful sins—and carried them on His back to Gethsemane. He withstood the excruciating pain of stakes through His wrists and feet. With blood streaming from His body, a piercing crown on His skull, rasping breath from His fluid-filled lungs, He was crucified just so you and I could have the joy and immense freedom of Jubilee. We celebrate our annual Jubilee on Easter—His resurrection from the dead.

When I see new growth edging through the hard ground, I think of it as a small reflection of Christ's return from the dead. What once seemed dead is now alive.

At Easter aren't you grateful for the promised renewal? Can you stop looking on the dingy dirt of winter past and release that to Jesus' promise of Jubilee? Will you accept the hope of new growth in your life, the hope that proclaims "that creation itself will be liberated from its bondage to decay and brought into the glorious freedom of the children of God" (Rom. 8: 21)?

MORE SCRIPTURE FOR STUDY:
Deuteronomy 15:1-11; Psalm 130;
Matthew 6:9-15; Ephesians 1:3-14

The Spacious Firmament

The spacious firmament on high,
With all the blue ethereal sky,
And spangled heavens, a shining frame,
Their great Original proclaim.
Th' unwearied sun, from day to day,
Does his Creator's powers display;
And publishes to every land
The work of an Almighty Hand.

Soon as the evening shades prevail
The moon takes up the wondrous tale,
And nightly to the listening earth
Repeats the story of her birth;
While all the stars that round her burn
And all the planets in their turn,
Confirm the tidings as they roll,
And spread the truth from pole to pole.

What though in solemn silence all
Move round the dark terrestrial ball?
What though no real voice nor sound
Amid their radiant orbs be found?
In reason's ear they all rejoice,
And utter forth a glorious voice,
Forever singing as they shine,
"The hand that made us is divine."

JOSEPH ADDISON

A NATIVE NEW ENGLANDER, Elizabeth Hoekstra lives on a farm in southern New Hampshire with her husband, Peter, and their two children. She holds an R.N. degree, with a concentration in psychology and maternal health, and has worked in both hospital and community health settings. Currently she manages Direct Path Ministries, which encourages women and families to form deeper interpersonal relationships under the lordship of Jesus Christ. Elizabeth also gardens, shows her horse Galilee, and enjoys skiing, boating, kayaking, biking, and hiking with her family.

Other Crossway books by Elizabeth M. Hoekstra

Keeping Your Family Close When Frequent Travel Pulls You Apart

Just for Girls

Just for Moms

A Season of Rejoicing

A Season of Grace

A Season of Gladness

With Mary Bradford
Chronic Kids, Constant Hope

MARLENE M^cLOUGHLIN WAS BORN IN BUFFALO, NEW YORK, and grew up in southern California. She received a degree in art history from Barnard College in New York City and a degree in drawing "with high distinction" from California College of Arts and Crafts.

In 1998 she went to Rome to work on her book *Road to Rome* (Chronicle Books) and decided to stay because of the beauty of the landscape and because dogs are allowed almost everywhere. She lives with Kiddo, a tortoise shell cat, and Barely, a German-Italian shepherd mix ... both pets are bilingual!

Marlene works from home on projects that vary from logo design to wall paintings. Her internationally award-winning books include: *Diane Seed's Rome for All Seasons, Across the Aegean,* and *The Passionate Observer.* Her clients include Linda Ronstadt, Williams-Sonoma, Ten Speed Press, and HarperCollins.

The typeface for this book is Adobe Garamond, originally designed by Claude Garamond in 1532. His oldstyle designs, based on the Aldine model, were the typefaces of choice in the composing rooms of printers well into the 18th century. In 1989 Robert Slimbach modified the design of this typeface slightly for Adobe, and it remains a favorite for book designers today.

The script used throughout is Escrita, a three weight, hand-drawn face designed by Mário Feliciano for T-26 in 1997.

The interior for this series was set by Joe Rosewell and Rose Graham.